ADDITIVE MANUFACTURING: A BEGINNER'S GUIDE

ADDITIVE MANUFACTURING

PRAYER RIJU R

Made with ♥ on the Notion Press Platform
www.notionpress.com

This book is dedicated to my father, Richard Stanly Y, whose unwavering support and guidance have been an inspiration to me throughout my life. His encouragement and belief in me have been the driving force behind my success. Without his constant love and support, this book would not have been possible.

Contents

Foreword

This book is intended for beginners who want to learn about the basics of additive manufacturing(AM). It covers the different types of AM technologies, materials, design principles, and the 3D printing process. It also discusses post-processing and finishing techniques, as well as the various industries that use AM and its future potential. The author provides a hands-on experience by providing examples and case studies of AM in different fields, making it easy for readers to understand and apply the concepts.

Preface

In this book, author Prayer Riju R, a Teaching cum Research Associate with hands-on experience in additive manufacturing technology, provides a comprehensive introduction to the field of additive manufacturing.

As a Teaching cum Research Associate in the field of additive manufacturing, the author brings a wealth of knowledge and experience to this book. The author's expertise in this field is evident in the way the book is written and the level of detail provided. The author's writing style is clear, concise, and easy to understand, making it accessible to both beginners and more experienced readers.

This book is a valuable resource for anyone interested in learning about additive manufacturing. Whether you're a student, engineer, designer, or hobbyist, this book will provide you with the knowledge and skills you need to understand and use this exciting technology. I highly recommend this book to anyone looking to learn about additive manufacturing and its potential to change the way we live and work.

Sincerely,

Prayer Riju R

Acknowledgements

First and foremost, I would like to thank the almighty for giving me the strength, knowledge, and inspiration to write this book

I would also like to express my gratitude to my research supervisor, Dr. Arulvel S, who has been a mentor, a guide, and a teacher. He provided me with the opportunity to work on cutting-edge technology and his guidance and expertise in writing have been invaluable in shaping my research.

I am also grateful to my mentor, Dr. Solomon Bobby S, for his invaluable guidance, and for providing me with the opportunity to explore my passion for additive manufacturing. His knowledge and experience in the field have been a great source of inspiration, and his support and encouragement have been instrumental in the completion of this book.

I would like to thank my institution, Vellore Institute of Technology, Vellore, for providing the resources and support necessary for my research and academic development. The opportunities and experiences that I have had at this institution have helped me to grow as a person and a professional.

I am also grateful to all the people who have supported me through this journey, including my colleagues, friends, and family. Your encouragement, feedback and support have been invaluable.

Finally, I would like to thank the readers of this book. Your interest and support are what motivate me to continue writing and sharing my knowledge and experience with others.

Thank you all for your support and encouragement.
Sincerely,
Prayer Riju

Prologue

Additive manufacturing, also known as 3D printing, is a rapidly advancing technology that has the potential to revolutionize many industries. The ability to create complex and customized parts, reduce costs, and improve efficiency is making additive manufacturing an essential technology in various fields. From aerospace, healthcare, and construction to food, fashion and personal products, Additive manufacturing is changing the way we design and manufacture products.

This book is intended for beginners who want to learn about the basics of additive manufacturing. It will cover the different types of AM technologies, materials, design principles, and the 3D printing process. It will also discuss post-processing and finishing techniques, as well as the various industries that use AM and its future potential. The book will provide a hands-on experience by providing examples and case studies of AM in different fields.

As a Teaching cum Research Associate in the field of additive manufacturing, I am excited to share my knowledge and experience with others. This book is the result of my years of research, experimentation, and hands-on experience in additive manufacturing.

The book is divided into chapters, each covering a different aspect of additive manufacturing, starting with the history of the technology and its evolution over time. We will delve into the different types of additive manufacturing technologies, the materials that are used, and the design principles that are essential to creating 3D models.

We will also discuss the 3D printing process, including the setting up and configuring of a 3D printer and the software that is used. We will also touch on the post-processing and finishing techniques that are used to create high-quality parts.

Throughout the book, we will look at the various industries that use additive manufacturing and explore the potential future applications of the technology.

This book is intended to provide a comprehensive introduction to additive manufacturing, making it accessible to beginners and those who are new to the field. I hope that it will inspire you to explore the exciting possibilities that additive manufacturing offers and that you will use this knowledge to create something new, innovative and groundbreaking.

Let's begin our journey into the world of additive manufacturing.

CHAPTER I

Overview of Additive Manufacturing (AM)

Additive Manufacturing (AM), also known as 3D printing, is a process of creating a physical object by adding successive layers of material. The object is built up layer by layer, using digital 3D models as a guide. This is in contrast to traditional manufacturing methods, such as subtractive manufacturing (e.g. CNC machining) or formative manufacturing (e.g. injection molding), which involve removing or shaping material to create an object.

AM has the ability to create complex geometries and shapes that would be difficult or impossible to produce using traditional manufacturing methods. It also allows for fast prototyping and low-volume production, making it a popular choice in industries such as aerospace, healthcare, and consumer products. Additionally, AM can also enable the creation of customized or one-of-a-kind products, as well as the use of new materials and combinations of materials.

There are several different types of AM technologies, each with their own set of advantages and limitations, including Fused Deposition Modeling (FDM), Stereolithography (SLA), Selective Laser Sintering (SLS), and Directed Energy Deposition (DED). Each technology uses different methods to create the object, such as by melting or curing a material, and requires specific materials and equipment.

CHAPTER II

History of AM and its evolution over time

The history of additive manufacturing (AM) can be traced back to the 1960s, when the first patent for a 3D printing-like process was filed by Dr. Hideo Kodama of Nagoya Municipal Industrial Research Institute in Japan. However, it wasn't until the 1980s that the first functional 3D printers were developed, using a process called stereolithography (SLA).

In the 1990s, new technologies such as Fused Deposition Modeling (FDM) and Selective Laser Sintering (SLS) were developed, and the first commercial 3D printers became available. These early machines were primarily used for prototyping and small-scale production in industries such as aerospace and automotive.

In the 2000s, advancements in technology and materials led to the development of more advanced 3D printing methods, such as Directed Energy Deposition (DED) and Binder Jetting. The cost of 3D printers also decreased, making them more accessible to small businesses and consumers.

In recent years, there have been significant advances in 3D printing technology, including the use of new materials such as metal, ceramics, and even living cells, as well as the development of multi-material and multi-color printing. The use of AM has also expanded to various industries such as healthcare, construction, and fashion.

As technology continues to advance and costs continue to decrease, AM is becoming an increasingly viable option for manufacturing a wide range of products, from small parts to large structures. It is expected to play a big role in the future of manufacturing and the Fourth Industrial Revolution.

CHAPTER III

Overview of the different types of Additive manufacturing technologies

There are several different types of additive manufacturing (AM) technologies, each with their own set of advantages and limitations. Some of the most common types of AM technologies include:

- **Fused Deposition Modeling (FDM):** This is a type of AM that uses a thermoplastic material that is extruded through a heated nozzle to create the object. The material is melted and extruded in a controlled manner, building up the object layer by layer. FDM is one of the most commonly used AM technologies, it's relatively low-cost, easy to use and it's able to print using a wide range of materials.
- **Stereolithography (SLA):** This is a type of AM that uses a laser to cure a liquid resin, solidifying it into a solid object. The laser is directed at specific points in the resin, curing the material in a precise manner, layer by layer. SLA is known for its high accuracy and surface finish and it's able to print using a wide range of materials, including clear and flexible materials.
- **Selective Laser Sintering (SLS):** This is a type of AM that uses a laser to heat and fuse a powdered material, building up the object layer by layer. The laser is directed at specific points in the powder, fusing the material together in a precise manner. SLS is known for its high accuracy and surface finish, and it's able to

print using a wide range of materials including metals, ceramics, and some plastics.

- **Directed Energy Deposition (DED):** This is a type of AM that uses a high-energy beam, such as a laser or an electron beam, to melt or vaporize material as it is deposited, building up the object layer by layer. DED is known for its ability to print complex geometries, and it's able to print using a wide range of materials including metals, ceramics, and some plastics.
- **Binder Jetting:** This is a type of AM that uses a binder to hold together a powdered material, building up the object layer by layer. The binder is selectively applied to the powder in a precise manner, bonding the material together in a controlled manner. Binder Jetting is known for its speed and ability to print large objects, and it's able to print using a wide range of materials including metals, ceramics, and some plastics.

These are the most common types of AM technologies, but there are many other types of AM technologies available, each with its own set of advantages and limitations.

CHAPTER IV

Comparison of the different additive manufacturing technologies and their advantages/disadvantages

Additive manufacturing (AM) technologies are constantly evolving, and each has its own set of advantages and disadvantages. Here is a comparison of some of the most common types of AM technologies and their advantages and disadvantages:

Fused Deposition Modelling (FDM)

Advantages

- A wide range of materials can be used
- Relatively low cost
- Easy to use
- Suitable for creating large objects
- Suitable for creating objects with relatively low accuracy

Disadvantages

- Poor surface finish
- Limited in the size and complexity of the object that can be printed

Stereolithography (SLA)

Advantages:

- High accuracy and surface finish
- A wide range of materials can be used

- Suitable for creating objects with intricate details

Disadvantages

- More expensive than FDM
- Materials are relatively fragile

Selective Laser Sintering (SLS)
Advantages

- High accuracy and surface finish
- Suitable for creating objects with intricate details
- A wide range of materials can be used, including metals and ceramics
- Suitable for creating large objects

Disadvantages

- Expensive
- Limited in the size and complexity of the object that can be printed
- Materials are relatively fragile

Directed Energy Deposition (DED)
Advantages

- Suitable for creating large and complex objects
- A wide range of materials can be used, including metals and ceramics
- Suitable for creating objects with intricate details

Disadvantages

- Expensive
- Poor surface finish
- Binder Jetting: Advantages:
- Suitable for creating large objects
- A wide range of materials can be used
- Suitable for creating objects with relatively low accuracy
- Fast printing process

Disadvantages

- Poor surface finish
- Limited in the size and complexity of the object that can be printed
- Materials are relatively fragile

It's important to note that this is not an exhaustive list, and that new technologies and developments in materials are continuously emerging. The best technology for a specific application will depend on the size, complexity, material and accuracy of the object, as well as the budget and the intended final use

CHAPTER V

Materials for Additive Manufacturing

Additive manufacturing (AM) uses a wide range of materials, including plastics, metals, ceramics, and composites. Here is an overview of some common materials used in AM:

1. Plastics: ABS, PLA, PETG, and Nylon are the most common plastics used in AM. These materials are relatively inexpensive, easy to work with, and have good thermal properties.
2. Metals: Stainless steel, titanium, aluminum, and gold are commonly used metals in AM. These materials are strong, durable, and heat-resistant, but can be more expensive than plastics.
3. Ceramics: Zirconia, alumina, and silicon carbide are common ceramics used in AM. These materials are hard, wear-resistant, and can withstand high temperatures, but can be brittle and difficult to work with.
4. Composites: Carbon fibre, glass fibre, and Kevlar are commonly used composites in AM. These materials are strong, lightweight, and can be used to create parts with unique properties, such as high strength or heat resistance.
5. Bioprinting: Hydrogels, collagen, and other biocompatible materials are used to print living cells and create functional tissue, such as bones, skin, and blood vessels.

6. Concrete and cement-based materials: These materials are used to print buildings and structures.
7. Wood-based materials: These materials are used to print wooden objects and structures

The choice of material will depend on the specific application of the printed object and the properties required. New materials are being developed and tested to be used in AM, such as graphene, and in the future, it is expected to have a wider range of materials for AM to choose from.

CHAPTER VI

3D Printing Process

The 3D printing process, also known as additive manufacturing, involves creating a physical object from a digital model by building it up layer by layer. The process can vary depending on the type of 3D printing technology being used, but here is a general overview of the steps involved in the 3D printing process:

1. Model creation: The first step in the 3D printing process is to create a digital model of the object that you want to print. This can be done using 3D modeling software such as Autodesk Fusion 360, SolidWorks, and SketchUp.
2. File preparation: Once the digital model is created, it needs to be prepared for printing. This includes checking the file format, scaling the model correctly, orienting the model correctly, checking the wall thickness, making sure the model is manifold and repairing any errors or defects.
3. Slicing: The next step is to slice the digital model into thin layers. This is done using slicing software, which takes the 3D model and generates the instructions for the printer to follow, layer by layer.
4. Printing: Once the digital model has been prepared, it is ready to be printed. The 3D printer reads the instructions from the slicing software and starts building the object layer by layer.
5. Finishing: Once the object is printed, it may require additional finishing steps such as sanding, polishing, or

painting to achieve the desired surface finish.

6. Post-Processing: After the object is printed and finished.

3d Printing process and parameters

The 3D printing process, also known as additive manufacturing, involves creating a physical object from a digital model by building it up layer by layer. The process and parameters can vary depending on the type of 3D printing technology being used, but here is a general overview of the process and parameters:

Process:

1. Model creation: The first step in the 3D printing process is to create a digital model of the object that you want to print. This can be done using 3D modeling software such as Autodesk Fusion 360, SolidWorks, and SketchUp.
2. File preparation: Once the digital model is created, it needs to be prepared for printing. This includes checking the file format, scaling the model correctly, orienting the model correctly, checking the wall thickness, making sure the model is manifold and repairing any errors or defects.
3. Slicing: The next step is to slice the digital model into thin layers. This is done using slicing software, which takes the 3D model and generates the instructions for the printer to follow, layer by layer.
4. Printing: Once the digital model has been prepared, it is ready to be printed. The 3D printer reads the instructions from the slicing software and starts building the object layer by layer.
5. Finishing: Once the object is printed, it may require additional finishing steps such as sanding, polishing, or

painting to achieve the desired surface finish.

Parameters:

1. Layer height: The thickness of each layer in the final print, which can range from 0.05 mm to 0.4 mm.
2. Infill: The density of the internal structure of the print, which can range from 0% (hollow) to 100% (solid).
3. Temperature: The temperature of the hotend and bed during the printing process, which can vary depending on the material being used.
4. Speed: The speed at which the print head moves during the printing process, which can be adjusted to optimize the balance between print quality and print time.
5. Cooling: The cooling of the print as it builds, which affects the final quality of the print, cooling fans can be adjusted to control the cooling rate.
6. Support: The support structure added to the model to ensure the overhangs can be printed properly, support structures can be added using slicing software.

By understanding the process and parameters, you can make adjustments to optimize the final quality of the print and reduce the risk

3D Printing software and slicers

3D printing software and slicers are essential tools for the additive manufacturing process. They are used to prepare the 3D model for printing and to control the 3D printer during the printing process. Here is an overview of the different types of 3D printing software and slicers:

3D Printing Software:

1. CAD (Computer-Aided Design) software: This type of software is used to create and manipulate 3D models. Examples include Autodesk Fusion 360, Solidworks, and SketchUp.
2. Slicing software: This type of software is used to slice the 3D model into layers that the 3D printer can understand. Examples include Cura, PrusaSlicer, and MatterControl.

Introduction to 3D modeling software

3D modeling software is a program that allows users to create and manipulate 3D models. These models can then be used for additive manufacturing (AM) or other purposes such as animation, simulation, and gaming. There are many different types of 3D modeling software available, each with its own set of features and capabilities. Here are some examples of popular 3D modeling software:

- Autodesk Fusion 360: This is a cloud-based 3D modeling software that is suitable for designing and engineering products. It provides a wide range of tools for creating 3D models, including parametric modeling, freeform modeling, and sculpting.
- SolidWorks: This is a popular 3D modeling software that is used in the engineering and manufacturing industries. It provides a wide range of tools for creating 3D models, including parametric modeling, sheet metal design, and mold design.
- Blender: This is a free and open-source 3D modeling software that is suitable for creating 3D models for animation, simulation, and gaming. It provides a wide range of tools for creating 3D models, including sculpting, texturing, and animation.

- SketchUp: This is a simple and easy-to-use 3D modeling software that is suitable for creating 3D models for architecture, interior design, and landscape design. It provides a wide range of tools for creating 3D models, including

Basic design principles for creating 3D models

When creating 3D models for additive manufacturing (AM), there are several basic design principles that should be taken into account:

1. Understand the limitations of the technology: Different AM technologies have different capabilities and limitations. For example, some technologies are better suited for printing complex geometries, while others are better for printing large objects. Understanding the capabilities and limitations of the technology you are using will help you make design decisions that are more feasible for AM.

2. Consider the orientation of the object: The orientation of the object during the printing process can have a big impact on the final product. For example, printing an object on its side can lead to a weaker structure or an object with a poor surface finish. Therefore, it is important to consider the orientation of the object during the printing process and design it accordingly.

3. Wall thickness: Wall thickness is an important consideration when creating 3D models for AM. It's important to ensure that the walls are thick enough to support the structure of the object, but not too thick that they take too long to print or use too much material.

4. Overhangs and supports: When creating 3D models for AM, overhangs and supports need to be taken into

account. Overhangs are any parts of the object that extend outwards and don't

File preparation for 3D printing

File preparation is an important step in the additive manufacturing (3D printing) process, as it ensures that the 3D model is ready for printing. Here are some basic steps for preparing a 3D model file for 3D printing:

1. File format: The 3D model file needs to be in a format that the 3D printer can read. The most commonly used file formats for 3D printing are STL and OBJ. Some printers also accept other formats such as VRML, PLY, and 3MF.
2. Scale: The 3D model file should be scaled correctly for the final printed object. This means that the dimensions of the model should be in the correct units of measurement (mm, cm, inches, etc.) and should match the desired size of the final printed object.
3. Orientation: The 3D model file should be oriented correctly for the printing process. This means that the object should be placed on the build plate in the correct orientation, taking into account any overhangs, supports, and the direction of the build.
4. Wall thickness: The 3D model file should be checked for appropriate wall thickness. Walls should be thick enough to support the structure of the object, but not too thick that they take too long to print or use too much material.
5. Manifold: The 3D model file should be manifold, which means that all edges are connected to two faces and there are no open edges or holes in the model. This is important for the printer to be able to create a solid

object.

6. File repair: If the 3D model file contains errors or defects, these should be repaired before printing. This can be done using various software tools such as Netfabb, MeshLab, and Meshmixer.

By following these basic steps for file preparation, you can ensure that the 3D model file is ready for 3D printing and will result in a better final product.

Slicers:

1. Cura: Cura is an open-source slicing software that is compatible with a wide range of 3D printers. It offers a user-friendly interface, a wide range of customization options and supports a variety of file formats.
2. PrusaSlicer: PrusaSlicer is a slicing software developed by Prusa Research. It offers advanced features such as multi-material printing, support for a wide range of file formats, and an easy to use interface.
3. MatterControl: MatterControl is a slicing software and 3D printing controller that allows users to remotely control their 3D printer, create custom profiles and monitor the print status.

It's important to note that some 3D printers come with their own proprietary slicing software, which may not be compatible with other 3D printers. So, it's always recommended to check the compatibility of the slicing software with the 3D printer before using it.

Setting up and configuring a 3D printer

Setting up and configuring a 3D printer can vary depending on the specific model and manufacturer, but here are some general steps for setting up and configuring a 3D printer:

1. Unpacking and assembly: The first step is to unpack the 3D printer and assemble it according to the manufacturer's instructions. This may include attaching the print bed, the extruder, and any other components.
2. Connecting to power and computer: Once the printer is assembled, it needs to be connected to a power source and a computer. This will typically involve connecting the printer to a power outlet and a USB cable to the computer.
3. Installing software: The next step is to install the necessary software on the computer. This may include the printer's driver software, slicing software, and any other software required to control and monitor the printer.
4. Calibration: After the software is installed, the printer needs to be calibrated. This may include leveling the print bed, adjusting the extruder's position, and setting the correct print temperature.
5. Loading filament: The next step is to load the filament into the extruder. This process can vary depending on the printer, but it generally involves loading the filament into the extruder's hotend and heating it to the correct temperature.
6. Test print: After the printer is calibrated and the filament is loaded, it's a good practice to run a test print to check that everything is working correctly. This will help you to identify and fix any issues before printing your final object.

CHAPTER VII

Design for Additive Manufacturing

Designing for additive manufacturing (AM) entails considering the technology's capabilities and limits, as well as the qualities of the materials being utilized. Here are some critical design considerations for producing 3D models for AM, with a focus on FDM printing:

1. Wall thickness: The walls of the object need to be thick enough to support the structure of the object, but not too thick that they take too long to print or use too much material. Wall thickness should be consistent throughout the object to ensure even cooling and contraction of the material.
2. Overhangs and supports: When designing 3D models for AM, overhangs, and supports need to be taken into account. Overhangs are any parts of the object that extend outwards and don't have any material underneath them. Supports are additional structures that are added to the model to support overhangs during the printing process.
3. Orientation: The orientation of the object during the printing process can have a big impact on the final product. For example, printing an object on its side can lead to a weaker structure or an object with a poor surface finish. Therefore, it is important to consider the orientation of the object during the printing process and design it accordingly.
4. File preparation: Proper file preparation is important to ensure that the model is ready for printing. This

includes ensuring that the file is in a format that the printer can read and that it is properly scaled and oriented for the printing process (STL file format, AMF, etc).

5. Material properties: Understanding the properties of the material being used is important when designing 3D models for AM. Materials have different shrinkage rates, thermal properties, and strength characteristics that can impact the final product(eg; PLA has less strength than ABS, but it is less expensive.).

6. Keep it simple: Simple designs are easier to print, less prone to errors, and faster to prepare for print. Avoid unnecessary details, and keep the design as simple as possible.

By keeping these design considerations in mind, you can create 3D models that are more suitable for AM and will result in a better final product

Troubleshooting common design issues in additive manufacturing

Additive manufacturing (AM) can present a number of design challenges that can affect the final product. Here are some common design issues in AM and ways to troubleshoot them:

1. Warping or curling: Warping or curling is caused by uneven cooling of the material during the printing process. This can be caused by a thin wall thickness or a large surface area. To troubleshoot this issue, increase the wall thickness or add more supports to the model.

2. Layer separation: Layer separation occurs when the layers of the printed object do not bond properly. This can be caused by a lack of adhesion between the layers

or by using a material with a low melting point. To troubleshoot this issue, try increasing the adhesion between the layers by adding a brim or a raft, or by using a material with a higher melting point.

3. Stringing: Stringing is caused by excess material being left between the printed object and the build plate. This can be caused by a nozzle that is too close to the build plate or by using a material that is too liquid. To troubleshoot this issue, try increasing the distance between the nozzle and the build plate or by using a material with a higher viscosity.

4. Overhangs and supports: Overhangs and supports can cause issues when creating 3D models for AM. Overhangs are any parts of the object that extend outwards and

CHAPTER VIII

Finishing and post-processing methods for 3D-printed parts

Finishing and post-processing 3D printed parts is an important step in the additive manufacturing process. It can help to improve the overall quality and appearance of the final product. Here are some common techniques for finishing and post-processing 3D-printed parts:

1. Sanding: Sanding is a common technique used to improve the surface finish of 3D printed parts. This can be done using sandpaper or abrasive pads of various grits, starting with a coarse grit and progressing to a fine grit.

2. Painting: Painting is another common technique used to improve the appearance of 3D printed parts. This can be done using paintbrushes or spray paint and can be used to create custom colors and designs.

3. Polishing: Polishing is a technique used to improve the surface finish of 3D printed parts. This can be done using polishing compounds and buffing pads.

4. Heat treatment: Heat treatment is a technique used to improve the mechanical properties of 3D-printed parts. This can be done by exposing the printed parts to high temperatures for a period of time.

5. Vapor smoothing: Vapor smoothing is a technique used to smooth the surface of 3D printed parts. This can be done by exposing the printed parts to a chemical vapor, such as acetic acid, which melts the surface of the

printed parts and smoothens it.

6. Tumbling: Tumbling is a technique used to deburr and smooth the surface of 3D-printed parts. This can be done by placing the printed parts in a tumbler with abrasive media.

7. Infilling: Infilling is a technique used to fill the internal structure of 3D printed parts, this can be done using different materials such as resin or epoxy to enhance the strength of the printed parts.

8. Coating: Coating is a process that involves applying a thin layer of material to the additively manufactured component to improve its properties. This can include adding a layer of chrome, a clear coat, or an anti-corrosion coating. The coating is typically used to improve the durability, corrosion resistance, and aesthetic appearance of the component.

By using these finishing and post-processing techniques, you can improve the overall quality and appearance of your 3D-printed parts. Always be aware of the material of your parts and the right finishing techniques that suit them. It's important to note that before applying any of these techniques, you should ensure that the surface of the additively manufactured component is cleaned and prepared properly to ensure the best adhesion of the coating or paint.

Troubleshooting common post-processing issues in additive manufacturing

Post-processing is an important step in the additive manufacturing process and can help to improve the overall quality and appearance of the final product. However, like any process, post-processing can present some issues. Here are some common post-processing issues in additive manufacturing and ways to troubleshoot them:

1. Warping or curling: Warping or curling can occur when the printed object cools unevenly. This can happen when the object is too large or has a thin wall thickness. To troubleshoot this issue, try heating the object to a higher temperature, or adding more supports to the model.

2. Surface roughness: Surface roughness can occur when the surface of the printed object is not smooth. This can happen when the object has not been sanded or polished properly. To troubleshoot this issue, try sanding or polishing the object using finer grits of sandpaper or polishing compounds.

3. Discoloration or color variations: Discoloration or color variations can occur when the object has not been painted or coated properly. This can happen when the paint or coating is not evenly applied or when the object is not cleaned properly before painting. To troubleshoot this issue, try cleaning the object thoroughly and apply the paint or coating evenly.

4. Adhesion issues: Adhesion issues can occur when the paint or coating does not adhere properly to the surface of the object. This can happen when the surface is not clean or when the paint or coating is not compatible with the material of the object. To troubleshoot this issue, try cleaning the surface thoroughly and using a paint or coating that is compatible with the material of the object.

5. Delamination: Delamination occurs when the layers of the printed object do not bond properly, leading to the separation of the layers. This can happen when the object is not heated properly

CHAPTER IX

Applications of Additive Manufacturing

Additive manufacturing (AM) has a wide range of applications across various industries. Here is an overview of the different industries that use additive manufacturing:

1. Aerospace and Defense: AM is used to create complex and lightweight parts for aircraft and spacecraft, such as engine components and structural parts.
2. Automotive: AM is used to create complex and lightweight parts for cars, such as engine components, transmission parts, and structural parts.
3. Healthcare: AM is used to create medical devices, such as prosthetic limbs and implants, as well as to produce customized surgical tools.
4. Architecture: AM is used to create architectural models and prototypes, such as building facades and structural components.
5. Consumer goods: AM is used to create a wide range of consumer goods, such as jewelry, fashion accessories, and household items.
6. Energy: AM is used to create complex and lightweight parts for wind turbines and other renewable energy systems.
7. Education: AM is used to create educational models and prototypes for engineering, design, and architectural students.

8. Food Industry: AM is used to create molds for chocolate, sugar and other food items, also to create intricate shapes and designs.
9. Industrial: AM is used to create tooling, fixtures, and end-use parts for industrial applications, such as machinery and equipment.
10. Art and Design: AM is used to create sculptures, jewelry, and other art and design pieces, as well as to produce customized molds and patterns.

AM is an emerging technology that is being used in many industries to create customized products, reduce costs, and improve efficiency. As technology continues to develop, it is expected to have an even greater impact on a wide range of industries.

Potential future applications of Additive Manufacturing

Additive manufacturing (AM), also known as 3D printing, is a rapidly advancing technology that has the potential to revolutionize many industries. Here are some potential future applications of additive manufacturing:

1. Bioprinting: AM is being used to create living tissue and organs, such as skin, bones, and blood vessels, which can be used for medical research, drug testing, and transplants.
2. Construction: AM is being used to create buildings and structures, such as houses and bridges, using a technique known as "contour crafting" or "3D printing of buildings."
3. Space exploration: AM is being used to create spacecraft and rocket parts, as well as to fabricate tools and equipment for use in space.

4. Robotics: AM is being used to create customized robotic parts and components, such as gears, actuators, and sensors.
5. Manufacturing: AM is being used to create tooling, molds, and end-use parts for a wide range of manufacturing applications, such as aerospace, automotive, and medical devices.
6. Personalized products: AM is being used to create customized products, such as prosthetic limbs, dental implants, and eyeglasses.
7. Food industry: AM is being used to create food items, such as pizzas and chocolate, with intricate shapes and designs.
8. Smart cities: AM is being used to create smart city infrastructure, such as traffic lights, and streetlights.
9. Pharmaceuticals: AM is being used to create customized pills, tablets, and capsules, with specific dosages and ingredients.
10. Fashion: AM is being used to create customized clothing and accessories, such as shoes and jewelry.

As technology continues to evolve, AM has the potential to revolutionize many industries and change the way we live and work. The future of AM is exciting and full of possibilities.

Future developments and advancements in Additive Manufacturing

Additive manufacturing (AM), also known as 3D printing, is a rapidly advancing technology that is continuously evolving and developing. Here are some future developments and advancements in additive manufacturing:

1. Materials: Development of new materials and composites that are compatible with AM processes. This will enable the printing of stronger, more durable and functional parts.
2. Multi-material printing: Advancements in multi-material printing will enable the printing of parts with different materials and properties in a single print job, resulting in more complex and functional parts.
3. High-speed printing: Advancements in print head technology and motion control will enable faster and more efficient printing, reducing the time and cost of production.
4. Large scale printing: Advancements in large scale printing technology will enable the printing of larger parts and structures, such as buildings and bridges.
5. Quality and accuracy: Improvements in scanning and metrology technology will enable more accurate and precise scanning and printing, resulting in higher-quality parts.
6. Automation: Automation and integration of AM into existing manufacturing processes, such as injection molding, will enable more efficient and cost-effective production.
7. Recycling: Development of recycling technology for AM, which will enable the recycling of materials and reduce waste during production.
8. Bioprinting: Advancements in bioprinting technology will enable the printing of living tissue and organs, such as skin, bones, and blood vessels, which can be used for medical research, drug testing, and transplants.
9. Remote Printing: Advancements in remote printing technology will enable printing from remote locations, such as space or other planets.

10. AI and machine learning: integration of artificial intelligence and machine learning in the AM process, will enable the optimization of the process, reducing the time and cost of production, and also improve the quality of the final product.

These advancements and developments in AM technology will enable the printing of more complex and functional parts, with better quality, faster and more cost-effectively. This will open new opportunities and possibilities in various industries, such as aerospace, healthcare, and construction.

CHAPTER X

Resources for further learning and exploration

There are many resources available for further learning and exploration of additive manufacturing (AM), also known as 3D printing. Here are a few options:

1. Online Courses: Websites such as Coursera, Udemy, and edX offer online courses on AM, covering topics such as 3D modeling, 3D printing technology, and design for AM.

2. Books: There are many books available on AM, covering a wide range of topics such as the history of AM, the different types of AM technologies, and design principles for AM. Some popular books include Additive Manufacturing - McGraw Hill by By C. P. Paul, A. N. Jinoop, "Additive Manufacturing Technologies (3D Printing, Rapid Prototyping, and Direct Digital Manufacturing" by Ian Gibson, David Rosen, and Brent Stucker, and "The Handbook of Additive Manufacturing Technologies" by John Barnes.

3. Online Communities and Forums: Websites such as Reddit, Thingiverse, and Instructables offer online communities and forums where users can share information, ask questions, and discuss different aspects of AM.

4. Professional associations: Professional associations such as the Additive Manufacturing Users Group (AMUG) and the American Society for Testing and Materials

(ASTM) offer resources such as workshops, conferences, and publications on AM.

5. Research papers: There are many research papers available on AM, covering a wide range of topics such as materials, processes, and applications of AM.

6. Industry events: Conferences and trade shows such as the International Manufacturing Technology Show (IMTS) and the Additive Manufacturing Conference & Exposition (AMCON) provide an opportunity to learn about the latest developments in AM technology and network with industry professionals.

7. Research centers and Labs: Many universities, research centers, and labs, such as the National Additive Manufacturing Innovation Institute (NAMII), Vellore Insitute of Technology(VIT), and the Massachusetts Institute of Technology (MIT), offer resources such as research opportunities, workshops, and tours.

By using these resources, you can gain a deeper understanding of AM, learn about the latest developments in the field, and connect with other professionals in the industry.